Healthy Camping Cookbook

Healthy, Quick, and Easy Campsite Recipes

Louise Davidson

CONTENTS

CONTENTS

INTRODUCTION

Have you ever come home from a camping trip to find that the whole family is craving salad, of all things? We have! What do you think it means?

For me, there was no question that this was our bodies' response to the combination of healthy fresh air and exercise coupled with the lax (and relaxed) menu of processed and junk foods we'd been splurging on while we were away. I realized we'd been filling up on hot dogs, hamburgers, macaroni salad, ice cream…and s'mores.

I knew we could do better, so I started looking into healthy recipes that wouldn't be too difficult to prepare at the campsite. I'm excited to share with you what I found. These recipes often have components you can choose to prepare at home to make life easier at the campsite, and they use a range of cooking methods that are fun and interesting:

- **Foil packs** – just grab an extra roll and pack it.
- **Skewers** – bamboo skewers are great. Remember to soak them in water first for about 30 minutes before using them.
- **Dutch oven** – If you don't have one, consider changing that!
- **Cast iron skillet** – our old friend. These pans can survive anything, even if we do sometimes need to re-season them when we get home.

In this cookbook, you will discover how to use these outdoor methods to prepare and serve a variety of meals you love to make at home. You'll be surprised how easy it is to make healthy versions of some of your favorite dishes like chicken cacciatore, butter chicken, and teriyaki steak skewers with a minimum of planning and effort, all at the campsite.

Our focus here is on healthy eating, so you'll see that we use a lot of vegetables, lean protein, whole grains, and healthy fats. We have recipes for paleo, dairy-free, and gluten-free diets, so no matter who's coming to the table, you'll have something for them!

CAMPSITE COOKING METHODS

In this cookbook, you will find that most recipes use one of these basic camping cooking methods:

- **Foil packets**
  Foil packet is a great cooking method for cooking outdoors. You only need to place your ingredients on a foil sheet, fold, seal, and cook to enjoy a quick and mess-free meal.

- **Grilling**
  Grilling is the most known cooking method for the outdoors. You just grill your meat, fish, and other ingredients until perfectly cooked and charred to your liking.

- **Dutch Oven**
  Cooking food in a cast iron Dutch oven is one of the easiest ways to cook during a camping trip as you do not need to check the state of the food all the time but just take care of the heat source, it being the campfire, charcoal or wood fire, propane stove, etc. The flavors develop over time and you can feed an army with one pot meals!

Foil Packets

The best thing about foil packet cooking is that it is extremely easy. You will quickly master all the techniques needed and you will use minimal tools in the process. Here are some of the basic things you need to know when it comes to preparing a foil packet meal for your campsite.

What You Need

Usually, a heat source, cooking spray, aluminum foil and some food are everything you need. Nothing more. **Always pick heavy-duty aluminum foil as this is better for foil packet cooking.** You need to fold it, and heavy-duty foil will hold up much better, and it is much handier to use it when you move your packet to the source of heat. This type of foil keeps all crimps and folds you made and you will be sure that all the steam and juices are held in the foil. It also comes in many width sizes. Depending on your family, pick one that will suit your needs.

Heat Sources

Any heat source will serve well for foil packet cooking, so you can use a grill, fire pit or propane source of heat. What you need to make sure of is not to place the foil packets you make directly on the flame. When using a fire pit or a grill, you want to prepare it by setting fire to some coals or wood. Let the fire burn down until the coals or wood are really hot but without open flame. Arrange the packets to cook so they are a few inches away from the heat source, and turn them occasionally for even cooking.

Cooking Sprays and Fats

Always make sure to spray the foil with cooking spray. You don't want your food to stick to the foil or get charred. The only situation when you can skip this step is if the food you are preparing already has enough oil to provide an adequate protective coating. Alternatives to cooking spray include melted butter or cooking oil; a light brushing of either of these is equally effective.

Feel Free to Experiment, But Keep Your Ingredients in Mind

When you start discovering the endless possibilities foil packet cooking offers, you will want to make your own packets. You should definitely try this, so feel free to experiment! There is one thing to keep in mind here, and that is the size and type of the ingredients you want to mix. For example, thin pieces of meat can only be combined with thinly sliced vegetables. You see, hard vegetables need longer cooking times, so if you mix them with thinly sliced meat, you will end up either undercooking the vegetables or overcooking the meat, simply because you put them both in one foil packet.

Always think of the cooking process when you choose your ingredients. Other good advice is to have at least one ingredient with a certain level of moisture, especially if the recipe you are creating is rather dry. In foil packet cooking, it's a tricky thing to add the ingredients once the cooking process has begun. This is why you need to be sure that you have made the right combination before you start. Tomatoes, marinades, and butter are examples of ingredients with moisture you can use.

Assembly

When you prepare your packets, keep in mind the variable cooking times for the ingredients you are using. The ingredients that need to be cooked the longest should be placed at the bottom of the foil, so they will have the most exposure to the source of heat.

Let's take an example. If you're combining meat with vegetables, a good choice is to put the meat to the bottom of the foil and then top it with vegetables, because meat demands longer cooking time. Another thing to note is the blending and texture of the ingredients you use. When you have an ingredient that will melt, like cheese, then put it nearest to the ingredient you want to mix it with so you can get the best flavor possible.

Styles of packets

You can choose between two different foil packet styles, depending on the ingredients you use when you prepare the packet.

The Flat Packet

This type of packet is tighter and keeps the ingredients closer together. It produces less steam and it is perfect for meals you want charred or seared. Note that less steam means less moisture in flat packets, which is why you need to be sure that you have enough ingredients with moisture and not only dry ingredients. Only when you are sure of this should you begin the cooking process. Trust me, just adding some butter is more than enough to make a difference between a juicy steak and the one that is dry and tough.

What you need to do to make a flat packet is take a sheet of aluminum foil and spray it on the inside. Lay the foil on a flat surface and put your ingredients in the middle, layering in accordance with the type and size of the ingredients. Do not spread out your ingredients too much. They should be compact and you will need some free surface around the outside foil edges.

Take two longer foil edges and fold them up to meet in the center. Then make large downward folds toward your ingredients. Bring the packet's short ends in toward the middle and crimp the foil to form a secure, tight packet. When putting the packet on your heat source, make sure to place the folded side up.

The Tent Packet

When you need more steaming and heat circulation, you should opt to use tent packets. Any packet that contains grains or produce will be better cooked in a tent packet. Actually, the only difference between the two styles is that there is more space between the top of the packet and the food, but this allows the food to steam.

Tent packets are made so the top doesn't touch your food. Leave about one to three inches of space above your ingredients. Use a large piece of heavy-duty aluminum foil (remember to spray it), and make sure it is big enough to fit all your ingredients. Allow more foil around the sides because you want enough space for airflow at the top. You also need enough left to make a secure crimp at the top.

Put your ingredients in the middle of the foil. Fold up the long ends of the foils over the food, meeting in the center a couple of inches above the ingredients. Use small folds to crease the foil until you are sure that its top is about three inches distant from the food. Crimp the top tightly. Bring in the sides just close enough to produce a strong seal on each side. When putting the packet over a heat source, place the folded side up.

Keep in Mind That You're Not at Home

We all feel at ease when cooking in our own kitchen, but this is not necessarily true when we are cooking outdoors. Cooking at a campsite is not the same as cooking in your kitchen, so you should always be prepared. You need to modify cooking times in accordance with the situation at that particular moment, and be aware that you can't always predict the time needed for cooking precisely. This is why the best idea is to buy a meat thermometer, which is the most reliable way of checking the temperature of the ingredients you are cooking inside the foil packets. We will discuss this more in the section on the food safety.

At-Home Preparation

The point of foil packet cooking is for everything to be simple at your campsite. If you prepare your food properly at home, you won't have to waste any time on it when you are at the site. There are people who like to prepare their foil packets at home, enabling them just to grill them at the campsite, and there are people who enjoy preparing the packet once they arrive at the site. Either way, here are some tips that will help you.

If you choose to prepare your packets ahead of time

Make sure to select solid fruits and vegetables, as well as other ingredients that hold their structure. Avoid ingredients that might get soggy when combined with juices, oils, and marinades.

Prepare your marinade in a separate container, rather than trying to mix the ingredients in the foil. Marinate the ingredients ahead of time. When marinating the ingredients and placing liquid seasonings into a foil packet, you need to make sure that folds and crimps are strong enough to hold them.

Always keep in mind your safety and think of how you will store foil packets before using them. Any packets that have dairy, fish, or meat should be kept cool. You can add additional protection by putting an assembled foil packet into a food storage bag. Label the bags clearly with the contents. This will enable you to avoid any cross-contamination if a foil packet leaks.

To partially assemble your packets at home

Food storage bags and jars for spices are something you will definitely want to use. You will find that numerous recipes in this book include spices. Don't plan to bring every spice jar you have at home. Instead, prepare a couple of blends of spices in advance and keep them in plastic food bags or jars. Note that it is not recommended for the spices to be stored in plastic bags for a long time, but if you just need to get through the weekend, you can use them without any worry.

Make sure to pre-cut and portion all of the ingredients, and use separate food bags or containers for each one. If you plan on using a lot of chopped onions, you can prepare an entire bag of them. Another good idea is to prepare sets of ingredients. For example, if you want to prepare a chicken and vegetable foil packet, then you can put sliced chicken in a marinade and spices in one storage bag and pre-cut vegetables in another bag. A neat trick is to label your bags, so you don't have to think what's in every one of them. You can also record which recipes you prepared the particular bag to be used for. Always keep food safety in mind.

To make things simpler, use some quality ingredients that were pre-made. For example, why waste time making a sauce when you can buy a great sauce and save yourself time and effort. There are also meals where canned ingredients are equally as good as the fresh ones. Also, you won't have to worry because you don't have to pay attention to keeping an appropriate temperature for safety, and they take less time to cook. To make you campsite cooking even easier, use precooked and quick cook items.

Prepare a couple of additional meals, just in case a recipe doesn't go the way it should, or if it should accidentally burn. This can also come in handy if you prolong your stay for another day or extra people show up for dinner!

Grilling

When camping, most parks and campground provide a fire pit with a grate. Those can be tricky as you don't know how well they have been cleaned and sometimes they look like they have been used since the caveman era! I like to bring my own portable barbecue grill. There are two main advantages in using a portable barbecue.

1. It's easy to set -up and you will be able to start cooking more quickly compared to starting a fire.
2. It's easier to adjust the cooking temperature and you will cook your food more evenly.

Grilling is one of the easiest methods to use to cook food outdoors be it in the backyard or at the campsite. The foundations are the same:

- Prepare your grate in advance by cleaning it thoroughly and oiling it so the food won't stick.
- Pre-heat your grill. If it's a charcoal grill, light it up about 30 minutes before you want to start cooking the food. well in advance to start cooking. For a propane barbecue, about 10 minutes will be enough to reach the desired temperature.
- If you have a temperature indicator, bring it to the temperature required before grilling.
- If the temperature cannot be controlled and becomes too hot, you can use aluminum trays to cook your food on. It will prevent over-cooking and charring your food.
- If you are using the campsite grate, it makes sense to use aluminum trays or at least an aluminum foil sheet on which you cook your food. It can prevent cross-contamination, rust particles mixing in with your food and makes it safer unless you can clean the grate thoroughly.

- Use long tongs and spatula as well as pot holders to protect your hands when manipulating the food being grilled.
- Bring a meat thermometer to make sure your food is cooked to the desired doneness.

Here is a practical chart for barbecue grilling time you can use for all your barbecue cooking for your favorite meats and poultry with some barbecue tips.

Barbecue Grilling Times

BEEF	Size	Grilling Time	Internal Temperature in °F (Fahrenheit)
Steaks	3/4" thick	3 to 4 min/side 4 to 5 min/side	Medium rare 145 Medium 160
Kabobs	1 inch cubes	3 to 4 min/side	145 to 160
Hamburger patties	1/2" thick	3 min/side	160
Roast, rolled rump (indirect heat) Sirloin tip (indirect heat)	4 to 6 lbs. 3 1/2 to 4 lbs.	18 to 22 min/lb. 20 to 25 min/lb.	145 to 160
Ribs, Back	cut in 1 rib portions	10 min/side	160
Tenderloin	Half, 2 to 3 lbs. Whole, 4 to 6 lbs.	10 to 12 min/side 12 to 15 min/side	Medium rare 145 Medium 160

PORK	Size	Grilling Time	Internal Temperature in °F (Fahrenheit)
Chops, bone in or boneless	3/4" thick 1 1/2" thick	3 to 4 min/side 7 to 8 min/side	145
Tenderloin	1/2 to 1 1/2 lbs.	15 to 25 min. total	145
Ribs (indirect heat)	2 to 4 lbs.	1 1/2 to 2 hrs.	145
Patties, ground	1/2" thick	4 to 5 min/side	145

HAM	Size	Grilling Time	Internal Temperature in °F (Fahrenheit)
Fully cooked (indirect heat)	any size	8 to 10 min/lb.	140
Cook before eating (indirect heat)	Whole, 10 to 14 lbs. Half, 5 to 7 lbs. Portion, 3 to 4 lbs.	10 to 15 min/lb. 12 to 18 min/lb. 30 to 35 min/lb.	160

LAMB	Size	Grilling Time	Internal Temperature in °F (Fahrenheit)
Chops, shoulder, loin, or rib	1" thick	5 min/side	145 to 160
Steaks, sirloin, or leg	1" thick	5 min/side	145 to 160
Kabobs	1" cubes	4 min/side	145 to 160
Patties, ground	4 oz., 1/2" thick	3 min/side	160
Leg, butterflied	4 to 7 lbs.	40 to 50 min. total	145 to 160

13

VEAL	Size	Grilling Time	Internal Temperature in °F (Fahrenheit)
Chops, steaks	1" thick	5 to 7 min/side	145 to 160
Roast, boneless (indirect heat)	2 to 3 lbs.	18 to 20 min/lb.	145 to 160

CHICKEN	Size	Grilling Time	Internal Temperature in °F (Fahrenheit)
Whole (indirect heat), not stuffed	3 to 4 lbs.	60 to 75 min.	165 to 180 as measured in the thigh
	5 to 7 lbs.	18 to 25 min/lb.	
	4 to 8 lbs.	15 to 20 min/lb.	
Cornish hens	18 to 24 oz.	45 to 55 min.	
Breast halves, bone in boneless	6 to 8 oz. each	10 to 15 min/side	165 to 170
	4 oz. each	7 to 8 min./side –	
Other parts: Legs or thighs	4 to 8 oz.	10 to 15 min/side	165 to 180
Drumsticks	4 oz.	8 to 12 min/side	
Wings,	2 to 3 oz.	8 to 12 min/side	

14

TURKEY	Size	Grilling Time	Internal Temperature in °F (Fahrenheit)
Whole turkey (indirect heat)	8 to 12 lbs. 12 to 16 lbs. 16 to 24 lbs.	2 to 3 hrs. 3 to 4 hrs. 4 to 5 hrs.	165 to 180 as measured in the thigh
Breast, bone in boneless	4 to 7 lbs. 2 3/4 to 3 1/2 lbs.	1 to 1 3/4 hrs. 12 to 15 min/side	165 to 170
Thighs, drumsticks (indirect heat) Direct heat (precook 1 hr.)	8 to 16 oz.	1 1/2 to 2 hrs. 8 to 10 min/side	165 to 180
Boneless turkey roll (indirect heat)	2 to 5 lbs. 5 to 10 lbs.	1 1/2 to 2 hrs. 2 to 3 1/2 hrs.	165 to 175

Tips for successful and safe barbecuing:

- To make sure that harmful bacteria, sometime present in uncooked meat and poultry, are destroyed during the cooking process, you must make sure that the internal temperature is high enough for safe consumption. Always use a meat thermometer inserted in the thickest part without touching any bones. Research from the U.S. Department of Agriculture (USDA) states that the color of the meat is not a dependable indicator meat or poultry has reached a temperature high enough to destroy harmful bacteria that may be present.

- Follow this chart for approximate cooking times, Outdoor grills can vary in heat.

- Use barbecue sauce during the last 15 to 30 minutes of grilling to prevent excess browning or burning resulting from the sugars of the sauce.

15

- USDA recommends cooking pork, beef, veal, lamb chops, ribs and steaks until it reaches a minimum internal temperature of 145°F and then let rest at least 3 minutes before slicing or consuming.

- Although it is safe to eat poultry with an internal temperature of 165°F, the flavors and the texture are best when the internal temperature reaches 170°F to 180°F

Source: Food Safety and Inspection Service, USDA

Cast Iron Dutch Oven

Choosing Your Cast Iron Dutch Oven

When it comes to purchasing a Dutch oven, you will find that you have many options to choose from. The choices may seem overwhelming. No matter what brands and price points you care to consider, there are some basic features to pay attention to when it comes to choosing your Dutch oven.

The first is size. A good size for a Dutch oven to take camping is 12-16 inches. Anything smaller than that may not allow you enough space to cook entire meals for multiple people. However, if you are a solo or couples-only camper, you may be able to get away with a smaller model. A 12-inch Dutch oven offers you enough room to prepare medium-sized meals. It fits in nicely at most campsite heat sources and is not so large and heavy that it becomes overly cumbersome to transport.

The next feature you want to look at when choosing a Dutch oven is the type of lid you prefer. Many manufacturers of Dutch ovens assume that they will be used primarily in the home and therefore can be missing some of the necessary features that you may need for cooking at your campsite. When choosing your Dutch oven, pick one that is not only tight fitting, but also has a bit of a concave curve to it, as well as at least a small rim around the edge. This will provide a stable surface for placing hot coals on top of your oven. Also, make sure that the lid has a solid handle that is large enough to be lifted with a lid lifter device.

Finally, choose a Dutch oven with good legs. It should have three evenly spaced legs that raise the oven at least an inch off of the ground. Good legs provide a stable cooking surface that allows plenty of room for hot coals to be placed underneath.

Cast Iron Dutch Oven How-To

Cooking with cast iron requires a few extra steps for maintenance, but there's no doubt that the results are worth it! Here are a few pieces of advice concerning care, upkeep, and use of your cast iron Dutch oven.

Seasoning your cast iron cookware

The first thing you need to know about cast iron care is seasoning. Seasoning is the process of applying oil to your cast iron, initially to remove contaminants, and then to prevent rust, corrosion, and baked-on food particles from degrading your cookware. The only time you ever need to use dish detergent on your cast iron is the first time you season it. To do that, scrub the inside and the outside of the oven with a hot, soapy mixture. Dry it thoroughly with a cloth, and then place it on a very hot heat source to finish drying the surface. Once it is completely dry, rub oil or fat (not butter) into the surface, both inside and out. Once the oven has been coated, take another cloth and continue to rub and polish the oven until it appears that there is no oily residue left. Place the oven back on the heat source for about an hour, flipping it over halfway through. Remove from the heat and let cool before handling. Depending on the oven, you may want to repeat this process several times before using it for the first time; repeated seasonings help to condition the cast iron and provide an attractive surface sheen. Season the oven again periodically throughout its life as you see fit.

Cleaning

Cleaning cast iron is a little different from cleaning other cookware. After using your Dutch oven, remove as much food from it as you can. While it's still warm, add about an inch or more of water and let it sit with the lid on. After 15–20 minutes, remove the lid and scrape off any remaining food bits. Discard the dirty water and repeat the process with clean water until the oven is free of food residue. Dry the inside thoroughly with a cloth and place the oven back on the warm coals to help drive off the remaining moisture. Once the oven is dry and cool, apply a very light layer of vegetable oil to the surface inside and out.

Cooking with a Cast Iron Dutch Oven at the Campsite

When using a cast iron Dutch oven at your campsite, you will usually be applying heat to both the top and the bottom by means of charcoal briquettes. The recipes in this book assume a temperature of approximately 350°F. In order to achieve this, you will use briquettes in numbers that are proportional to the size of your oven. A general rule is to use at least twice as many briquettes as the diameter of your oven. For example, if you have a 12-inch oven, you will use 24 pieces of charcoal. A 16-inch oven would require approximately 32. This, however, is a very generalized rule that should only serve as a guideline and will also depends on the temperature you want to cook your food as you will see in the table below. Always use a thermometer when you are learning to gauge the temperature of your oven, especially if you are using wood rather than coals.

Here is a table that gives you a general idea of the number of hot coals you will need according to the size of your cast iron Dutch oven and the desired cooking temperature.

Dutch Oven Temperature Chart
Number of Charcoal Briquettes Required

Temp.→ Oven Size ↓	325°F 163°C	350°F 177°C	375°F 191°C	400°F 204°C	425°F 218°C	450°F 232°C
8 inches	Top: 10 Bottom: 5 Total: 15	Top: 11 Bottom: 5 Total: 16	Top: 11 Bottom: 6 Total: 17	Top: 12 Bottom: 6 Total: 18	Top: 13 Bottom: 6 Total: 19	Top: 14 Bottom: 6 Total: 20
10 inches	Top: 13 Bottom: 6 Total: 19	Top: 14 Bottom: 7 Total: 21	Top: 16 Bottom: 7 Total: 23	Top: 17 Bottom: 8 Total: 25	Top: 18 Bottom: 9 Total: 27	Top: 19 Bottom: 10 Total: 29
12 inches	Top: 16 Bottom: 7 Total: 23	Top: 17 Bottom: 8 Total: 25	Top: 18 Bottom: 9 Total: 27	Top: 19 Bottom: 10 Total: 29	Top: 21 Bottom: 10 Total: 31	Top: 22 Bottom: 11 Total: 33
14 inches	Top: 20 Bottom: 10 Total: 30	Top: 21 Bottom: 11 Total: 32	Top: 22 Bottom: 12 Total: 34	Top: 24 Bottom: 12 Total: 36	Top: 25 Bottom: 13 Total: 38	Top: 26 Bottom: 14 Total: 40
16 inches	Top: 25 Bottom: 12 Total: 37	Top: 26 Bottom: 13 Total: 39	Top: 27 Bottom: 14 Total: 41	Top: 28 Bottom: 15 Total: 43	Top: 29 Bottom: 16 Total: 45	Top: 30 Bottom: 17 Total: 47

By no means is this chart an exact science! But it gives a good indication of the cooking temperature according to the size of cast iron Dutch oven you are using and the number of coals you will approximately need. Remember to replenish as the coals cool down, especially if you are preparing a dish that requires several hours of cooking.

With wind, more oxygen is added to the cooking environment, which causes coal to emit more heat at once, shortening its burning time. Wind can also blow away the heat, so it'd be wise to block the wind around the Dutch oven when it's windy. This can be done with aluminum foil, rocks, logs, there are even stove windscreens and camping tables tailored for this purpose, among others.

The ground is another factor to keep in mind. Moist cold ground takes heat away and can even extinguish the charcoal. Setting up a dry surface below the charcoal to keep it unaffected by the ground is the way to go.

The colder the air is, it's more difficult to heat the Dutch oven. It's the same with higher elevation (due to air density) and humidity. More sunlight means more to be absorbed and turned into heat, especially when the cast iron Dutch oven is black due to the color's properties. When it's really warm, the sunlight can even be too much, so covering it with a camping canopy is a good idea, and it can also serve from guarding the charcoal against the rain. When it's too humid to light the charcoal briquettes, you may need to use a chimney starter.

While the above table is for the cast iron Dutch oven, both it and the aluminum version have their advantages and disadvantages. Aluminum Dutch ovens are a third of the weight of the cast iron ones. They also do not rust, are easy to clean and heat up more quickly, requiring about ¾ as much coal than their cast iron counterparts. Cast iron Dutch ovens, on the other side, retain heat longer and distribute it more evenly, which is often desired for preparing food.

Placement of the coals on the bottom and/or lid

Where you place the coals, and in what numbers, also depends on the method of cooking. Different quantities and configurations can help distribute the heat properly or concentrate it to a critical area. For sautéing, boiling, frying, or open lid cooking, you will place all of the coals underneath the oven. For methods of cooking that require both a top and bottom heat source, distribute the coals between the bottom and the top of the lid. Depending on the proportion of heat that you need from each heat source, you can divide them up with half on top and half on the bottom, or ¾ on the bottom and ¼ on top. Give yourself a little time to practice adjusting the heat on your Dutch oven before creating more involved meals. Here is a general guideline depending on the cooking method you are using.

21

1. **For roasting**, coal in the Dutch oven should be split evenly between top and bottom.
2. **For baking**, ¾ should be on top and ¼ on the bottom.
3. **For simmering and stewing**, 4/5 should be on top, and 1/5 on the bottom.
4. **For frying and boiling**, all coals should be on the bottom part.

To check the temperature of the food, use an instant-read meat thermometer easily available online and in kitchen supply stores. If you happen to forget a thermometer or just don't want to use one, you can also rely on your sense of smell. Generally speaking, if the food doesn't emit anything that you can smell, it is not done, and if it smells burnt, it is burning or starting to, time to take it off the heat and hope it's not all burned. If it smells really good and profusely, it's probably done or nearly so.

Cooking with your Dutch oven outside is a little different from using it indoors, and it requires a few pieces of additional equipment. First of all, you definitely want a good, reliable lid lifting device. Cast iron can get very hot, especially if you have hot coals placed on the lid. To protect yourself from burns, use a heat protective glove or mitt along with a lid lifting device to remove the lid. A lid stand is also a good idea. This will provide a heat-proof resting place for your lid so you won't have to set it down on the dirty ground. You may also find a long pair of tongs helpful for moving hot coal briquettes. If you spend a great deal of time cooking in the great outdoors, at some point you may wish to invest in either a tripod or a Dutch oven cooking table. These devices are a little more cumbersome than the Dutch oven alone, but they provide a more stable, safer cooking environment.

BREAKFAST

Healthy Carrot Cake Pancakes

These wholesome pancakes taste like dessert, but they're low in calories and have healthy fiber and protein. (Tip: Serve with a slice of fresh or grilled pineapple!)

Serves 6 | Prep. time 10 min. | Cooking time 20 min.

Ingredients
1 cup all-purpose flour
¼ cup flax meal
¼ cup chopped walnuts
2 teaspoons baking powder
1 teaspoon ground cinnamon
¼ teaspoon salt
⅛ teaspoon ground nutmeg
⅛ teaspoon allspice
⅛ teaspoon ground ginger
¼ cup brown sugar
¾ cup low-fat buttermilk
1 tablespoon canola oil
1 ½ teaspoons vanilla extract
2 large eggs, lightly beaten
3 tablespoons butter, softened
2 tablespoons honey
1 ½ cups finely grated carrot

Directions

1. At home, in a resealable bag, combine the flour, flax meal, walnuts, baking powder, cinnamon, salt, nutmeg, allspice, and ginger.
2. In a mason jar (or other leakproof container) combine the brown sugar, buttermilk, oil, vanilla, and eggs. Be sure to keep this mixture chilled.
3. Combine the butter with the honey and place it in a small container.
4. When you are ready to make the pancakes, empty the dry ingredients into a mixing bowl and fold in the grated carrots. Add the wet ingredients and mix until just combined.
5. Heat a cast iron skillet or Dutch oven over medium heat. Coat it with cooking spray, and ladle in the batter a quarter cup at a time.
6. Cook until the bottom is firm and bubbles appear on the top, then flip and cook until the bottom is lightly brown.
7. Serve with a dab of honey butter.

Nutrition per serving (2 pancakes)
Calories 310, Fat 13.3 g, Carbs 39.8 g, Sugar 37.6 g,
Protein 7.8 g, Sodium 381 mg

Egg White Omelet

These healthy omelets dish out a serving of vegetables and 10 grams of protein! Serve with a slice of whole grain toast if you like, or a piece of fruit.

Serves 4 | Prep. time 5 min. | Cooking time 20 min.

Ingredients
8 large egg whites
½ teaspoon salt
¼ teaspoon freshly ground black pepper
½ cup green onion, chopped
½ cup firm cherry tomatoes, halved
½ cup spinach, chopped
1 tablespoon olive oil
2 tablespoons grated Parmesan cheese

Directions
1. Place a skillet over medium heat.
2. Combine two of the egg whites in a mixing bowl, and whisk until frothy. Stir in a quarter of the salt and pepper, green onion, cherry tomatoes, and spinach.
3. Heat a quarter of the oil in the pan, and pour in the egg mixture. Be very mindful of the heat, and lift the skillet off the coals or stove if the egg is browning too quickly.
4. As the egg sets, lift the edge of the omelet with the spatula, and allow the uncooked egg to go under the cooked portion. When it's nearly set, flip it over.
5. Sprinkle the top with half a tablespoon of the Parmesan. Fold the omelet in half, and cook until golden and cooked through.
6. Repeat for each serving.

Option! You can poach these by placing all the ingredients for individual omelets in sturdy resealable bags (one bag = one omelet) and dropping them in simmering water until the eggs are set. This way, you don't need the oil for frying, and you can prepare more than one at a time. Just add the Parmesan to the egg mixture, or sprinkle it over the finished omelet.

Nutrition per serving
Calories 75, Fat 3 g, Carbs 4 g, Sugar 3 g,
Protein 9.4 g, Sodium 230 mg

Quinoa Peach Breakfast

This wholesome breakfast is delicious warm, but you can also make it in mason jars at home and keep it in the cooler.

Serves 6 | Prep. time 10 min. | Cooking time 30 min.

Ingredients
2 cups water
1 cup quinoa
½ teaspoon cinnamon
1 tablespoon coconut oil
Pinch of salt
2 cups plain 2% Greek yogurt
2 large ripe peaches, chopped
4 tablespoons natural almond butter, divided
4 teaspoons honey, divided

Directions
1. Bring the water to a boil over high heat. Rinse the quinoa and add it to the pot with the cinnamon, coconut oil, and salt.
2. Reduce the heat and simmer until the quinoa is cooked, about 30 minutes.
3. Divide the quinoa into four serving bowls. Top each with half a cup of Greek yogurt, half a chopped peach, a tablespoon of almond butter, and a teaspoon of honey.

Nutrition per serving
Calories 379, Fat 17.0 g, Carbs 42.1 g, Sugar 17.5 g, Protein 18.0 g, Sodium 61.2 mg

Turkey Bacon Breakfast Casserole

Warm up your Dutch oven and layer in some basic ingredients to make this filling and nutritious breakfast.

Serves 6 | Prep. time 10 min. | Cooking time 40 min.

Ingredients
1 tablespoon olive oil
12 slices turkey bacon, chopped
1 large sweet potato, shredded
1 onion, chopped
1 red bell pepper, chopped
2 cups baby spinach
12 eggs, beaten
½ cup sharp Cheddar cheese, shredded
½ cup green onion, chopped

Directions
1. Place your Dutch oven over medium heat, about 15 briquettes. Oil the inside lightly, or line it with aluminum foil and oil that.
2. Warm the oil and cook the turkey bacon until it begins to crisp up. Add the sweet potato and stir. Spread this layer over the bottom of the pot, but don't pack it down.
3. Layer on the onion and red bell pepper.
4. Beat the eggs until they are well combined, and stir in the spinach. Pour this mixture over the vegetables.
5. Arrange the Dutch oven with 12 briquettes underneath and 15 on top. Cook for 30–40 minutes, until the eggs are set. In the final 5 minutes, sprinkle on the cheese and green onion.

Nutrition per serving
Calories 293, Fat 19.1 g, Carbs 9.9 g, Sugar 2.9 g,
Protein 20.2, Sodium 485.1 mg

Shakshuka

This zesty tomato sauce with eggs will have your morning taste buds singing.

Serves 6 | Prep. time 10 min. | Cooking time 25 min.

Ingredients
1 red pepper, cored and diced
1 small onion, diced
2 cloves garlic, minced
½ teaspoon pepper
¼ teaspoon salt
¼ teaspoon paprika
¼ teaspoon chili powder
Pinch of cayenne powder
2 (28-ounce) cans diced tomatoes
½ teaspoon chili-garlic paste
2 tablespoons tomato paste
2 teaspoons olive oil
6 eggs
¼ cup green onion, chopped

Directions
1. If you like, you can prepare some of this recipe at home. Chop the red pepper, onion, and garlic, and place them in a resealable bag.
2. Combine the pepper, salt, paprika, chili powder, and cayenne pepper with the chili garlic paste and tomato paste in a small container, and seal it tightly.
3. At the campsite, place a skillet over medium heat.
4. Heat the oil and cook the vegetable mixture for 3–4 minutes, until the onions are softened.

5. Pour in the tomatoes and the spice mixture, and stir to combine. Let it heat up and cook for about 10 minutes, to let the liquid evaporate somewhat.
6. Crack the eggs onto the sauce, but do not stir. Cover the pan and cook for about 5 minutes, until the eggs are cooked to your liking.
7. Serve with a sprinkle of green onion.

Nutrition per serving
Calories 132, Fat 6.9 g, Carbs 11.1 g, Sugar 2.2 g, Protein 8.2 g, Sodium 224 mg

Whole Grain Blueberry Bread Pudding

This all-time favorite is cooked in a foil packet. You can make one large pudding or individual sizes to suit your campers. Feel free to customize with other fruits!

Serves 4 | Prep. time 35 min. | Cooking time 30–40 min.

Ingredients
2 eggs
1 cup 1% milk
½ cup sugar
1 teaspoon vanilla extract
4 cups whole-grain bread cubes
1 cup blueberries

Directions
1. Beat the eggs with the milk, sugar, and vanilla.
2. Stir in the bread cubes and blueberries, and let the mixture soak for 30 minutes.
3. Meanwhile, set out your foil sheets and coat them lightly with oil or cooking spray.
4. Place the bread mixture in the foil, and fold it to form a tent with room for steam.
5. Cook over indirect heat, turning from time to time, for 30–40 minutes.

Nutrition per serving
Calories 325, Fat 5.4 g, Carbs 57.7 g, Sugar 35.4 g, Protein 13.0 g, Sodium 278 mg

Banana Paleo Pancakes

With just a few ingredients, you can set your campers up for a happy, busy morning outdoors.

Serves 6 | Prep. time 5 min. | Cooking time 10–12 min.

Ingredients
2 tablespoons coconut oil
6 ripe bananas
6 eggs
½ cup almond butter
2 teaspoons cinnamon
½ teaspoon salt

Directions.
1. Place a cast iron skillet over medium heat.
2. Mash the bananas very well, and beat in the eggs until smooth.
3. Stir in the almond butter, cinnamon, and salt.
4. Melt a little of the coconut oil in the skillet and spoon in some batter. Keep the pancakes small so they'll be easy to flip.
5. Cook for 2–3 minutes on each side.
6. Repeat until all the pancakes are cooked

Nutrition per serving (2 pancakes)
Calories 346, Fat 21.3 g, Carbs 32.4 g, Sugar 15.6 g, Protein 10.7 g, Sodium 381 mg

SANDWICH AND WRAPS

Light Philly Cheese Wraps

The flavor you love, the protein you need – without a load of excess fat and calories.

Serves 4 | Prep. time 20 min. | Cooking time 20–25 min.

Ingredients
1 tablespoon olive oil
1 small onion, sliced
6 mushrooms, sliced
1 green pepper, sliced
10 ounces leftover roast beef, thinly sliced (deli can be used but it's higher in salt and preservatives)
4 (10-inch) whole wheat tortillas
2 tablespoons butter
½ teaspoon garlic powder
4 ounces provolone cheese, sliced

Directions
1. In a skillet over medium heat, warm the oil.
2. Sauté the onion, mushrooms, and green pepper until soft. (If you are doing this step at home, let them cool. Transfer them to a resealable bag and refrigerate them.)
3. At the campsite, set out a 4 pieces of aluminum foil and coat them with cooking spray.
4. Combine the butter with the garlic powder, and spread it on the tortillas.

5. Arrange the meat slices on the bread, and top with the vegetable mixture and cheese.
6. Roll up the wraps and wrap them in the foil. Cook over indirect heat for about 10 minutes, turning it from time to time, until the bread is warm and the cheese is melted.

Nutrition per serving
Calories 444, Fat 23.6 g, Carbs 28.2 g, Sugar 4.3 g,
Protein 31.4 g, Sodium 846.4 mg

Black Bean Burritos

Wrap these healthy and delicious burritos in foil and toast them near the fire! You can prepare the filling at home if you like, and just roll and heat them at the campsite.

Serves 6 | Prep. time 20 min. | Cooking time 15 min.

Ingredients
1 tablespoon vegetable oil
1 small onion, chopped
1 small red bell pepper, chopped
½ small green bell pepper, chopped
2 cloves garlic, minced
2 (15-ounce) can black beans, rinsed and drained
1 jalapeño pepper, minced
6 ounces low fat cream cheese
1 teaspoon salt
Pinch red pepper flakes
¼ cup chopped fresh cilantro
6 (10 inch) flour tortillas

Directions
1. In a skillet over medium heat, warm the oil.
2. Sauté the onion, bell peppers, and garlic until softened, about 3 minutes.
3. Add the beans, jalapeño, cream cheese, salt, and red pepper flakes.
4. Remove the skillet from the heat and stir in the cilantro.
5. If you're preparing this ahead, cool and refrigerate the mixture in a lidded container or resealable bag.

6. When you're ready to serve, divide the mixture among the tortillas.
7. Spray sheets of foil with cooking spray, and wrap the burritos tightly. Heat them near the coals, turning occasionally, until heated through, about 15 minutes.

Nutrition per serving
Calories 486, Fat 13.2 g, Carbs 72.5 g, Sugar 2.0 g,
Protein 20.1 g, Sodium 817.9 mg

Barbecue Pulled Chicken Burgers

Chicken is great choice for this delicious, drippy sandwich because it's leaner and cleaner than pork. Load on some delicious slaw and dig in! Also, you can serve these in Bibb lettuce leaves if you'd like to skip the bread.

Serves 6 | Prep. time 15 min. | Cooking time 1 hour 15 min.

Ingredients
2 teaspoons olive oil
1 ½ pounds boneless, skinless chicken (breasts and or thighs, or a mix)
1 small onion, chopped
1 cup prepared barbecue sauce
½ cup water
1 teaspoon paprika
½ teaspoon chili powder
1 teaspoon black pepper
6 large whole wheat buns

For the slaw
¼ cup non-fat Greek yogurt
1 tablespoon sugar
1 tablespoon vinegar
1 ½ cups slaw mix (cabbage and carrot)

Directions
1. In a Dutch oven over medium heat (15–18 briquettes), warm the oil. Brown the chicken on both sides. Remove the chicken to a plate and cover.
2. Sauté the onion until softened, about 3 minutes. Add the chicken pieces back to the pot, together with the barbecue

sauce, chicken broth, paprika, chili powder, and black pepper.

3. Cover the Dutch oven, and cook for one hour with 12 briquettes underneath and 6 on top. The temperature should be around 300°F.

4. Meanwhile, prepare the slaw. Combine the yogurt with the sugar and vinegar, and then fold in the cabbage mixture.

5. Remove the lid after an hour and take out the chicken. Shred it with forks.

6. Allow the liquid to reduce, if necessary. Add the chicken back to the sauce and stir until it's nice and thick.

7. Serve the meat on the buns with a big spoonful of slaw.

Nutrition per serving
Calories 338, Fat 8.3 g, Carbs 35.1 g, Sugar 20.2 g, Protein 31.6 g, Sodium 636 mg

Asian Chicken Lettuce Wraps

These light and tasty wraps are very customizable. Choose your favorite fillings and dig in! If you like, you can prepare the chicken at home and bring it along.

Serves 4 | Prep. time 10 min. plus 30 min. marinating time | Cooking time 15 min.

Ingredients
For the marinade
¼ cup orange juice
3 tablespoons low-sodium soy sauce
2 tablespoons brown sugar
1 tablespoon sesame oil
1 tablespoon minced fresh garlic
1 tablespoon orange zest
¼ teaspoon red pepper flakes pepper

1 pound boneless skinless chicken breast, thinly sliced
2 teaspoons vegetable oil
2 cups brown rice, cooked
12 Bibb lettuce leaves
1 teaspoon sesame seeds
4 green onions, diagonally sliced

Optional toppings:
Sliced cucumbers, radish, tomatoes, jalapeño peppers

Directions

1. In a resealable bag, combine the orange juice, soy sauce, brown sugar, sesame oil, garlic, orange zest, and red pepper flakes. Mix well, and remove 3 tablespoons to a small bowl. Set it aside.
2. Add the chicken to the bag and manipulate it so it's all coated. Keep it in the fridge or the cooler for at least 30 minutes.
3. In a skillet over medium heat, warm the oil.
4. Remove the chicken from the marinade and discard the marinade.
5. Sauté the chicken until it is nicely browned. (To prepare ahead, cool the chicken and place it in a clean bag with the reserved sauce. Keep it cold or frozen until you need it.)
6. To prepare the wraps, warm the rice (and the chicken, if it's cold).
7. Set out the lettuce leaves. Into each, put 3 tablespoons of brown rice and a portion of the chicken. Sprinkle with sesame seeds, and top with the green onions and other desired toppings.

Nutrition per serving

Calories 298, Fat 7.3 g, Carbs 27.1 g, Sugar 2.6 g,
Protein 29.4 g, Sodium 209.1 mg

Portobello Mushroom Burger

Even the beef lovers on your campout will enjoy this satisfying burger. The crisp, cool vegetables complement the deep flavor of the mushrooms beautifully.

Serves 4 | Prep. time 5 min. plus 30 min. marinating time | Cooking time 7 min.

Ingredients
4 large portobello mushroom caps

For the marinade
2 tablespoons balsamic vinegar
1 tablespoon low-sodium soy sauce
1 tablespoon olive oil
1 teaspoon steak seasoning
1 teaspoon dried tarragon

4 ounces light Swiss cheese
4 whole wheat hamburger buns

Suggested toppings:
Sliced red onion, tomato, avocado, lettuce, pickle

Directions
1. Arrange the mushroom caps on a plate. Combine the ingredients for the marinade and drizzle it over the mushrooms. Let them sit for half an hour, turning them occasionally.
2. Heat your grill to medium and cook the mushrooms for 6–7 minutes, turning them from time to time and basting them with the marinade.

3. When they are almost done, place one ounce of Swiss cheese on each.
4. Make your burgers with your favorite toppings, and enjoy.

Nutrition per serving

Calories 275, Fat 11.7 g, Carbs 29.7 g, Sugar 2.0 g, Protein 16.1 g, Sodium 620.2 mg

SOUPS AND STEWS

Chili Con Carne

This recipe is a perfect choice for cold-weather camping, or those rainy days we all get sometimes.

Serves 6 | Prep. time 10 min. |
Cooking time 1 hour and 10 min.

Ingredients
Spice packet
1 teaspoon salt
½ teaspoon freshly ground black pepper
2 ½ teaspoons ground cumin
1 ½ teaspoon chili powder
1 teaspoon crushed chilies
1 tablespoon paprika
1 tablespoon dried oregano
1 cinnamon stick
1 bay leaf

1 ½ pounds lean ground beef
1 large onion, chopped
3 cloves garlic, chopped
2 (14.5-ounce) cans diced tomatoes with liquid
1 (15-ounce) can red kidney beans, rinsed and drained
1 (15-ounce) can black beans, rinsed and drained

Directions

1. At home, combine the necessary spices in a lidded container or resealable bag.
2. At the campsite, place your 12-inch Dutch oven over 18 briquettes.
3. Sauté the ground beef until it is browned and drain any excess grease.
4. Add the onion and cook until it is tender, then stir in the garlic. Add the spices and tomatoes.
5. Cover the pot, and arrange it with 16 briquettes underneath and 8 on top. Cook for 45 minutes, maintaining a temperature around 325°F.
6. Add the beans and cook for 15 more minutes. Remove the cinnamon stick and bay leaf before serving.

Nutrition per serving

Calories 318, Fat 12.4 g, Carbs 30.1 g, Sugar 7.5 g,
Protein 19.4 g, Sodium 1020 mg

Campfire Chicken and Dumplings

This is a super simple, super tasty version of the home classic. The dumplings are made with whole wheat flour and are guaranteed to please.

Serves 6 | Prep. time 10 min. | Cooking time 45 min.

Ingredients
1 whole fryer chicken, 4-5 pounds
4 stalks celery, sliced
1 large onion, diced
2 medium carrots, peeled and sliced
1 teaspoon salt
1 teaspoon black pepper
2 teaspoons garlic powder
1 (14.5-ounce) can low-sodium chicken broth

For the dumplings
1 ½ cups white whole wheat flour
½ teaspoon salt
5 tablespoons butter
1 egg
½ cup milk
1 tablespoon dried parsley

Directions
1. Place a large Dutch oven over 18–20 briquettes. Add the chicken with enough water to just cover. Put in the celery, onion, carrots, salt, black pepper, and broth.
2. Bring the pot to a boil and then transfer it to less intense heat. Keep it simmering for an hour.

45

3. Meanwhile, prepare the dumpling batter. Combine the flour and salt and cut in the butter. Mix in the egg, milk, parsley, and pepper, and knead for about 5 minutes.
4. Carefully remove the chicken to a strainer and let it cool a little. Remove and discard any skin and fat, and pull the meat from the bones.
5. Skim the fat from the broth and add the cooked chicken back in. Taste the broth and add more seasonings if desired.
6. Pull off little bits of the dumpling dough and roll them into balls if desired. Drop them into the broth.
7. Cover the pot and bring it to a simmer. Cook, covered, for 20 minutes.

Nutrition per serving

Calories 463, Fat 16.3 g, Carbs 25.2 g, Sugar 3.4 g, Protein 50.1 g, Sodium 940.6 mg

Hodge Podge

We make hodge podge when the new potatoes are out—and this is why it's a perfect recipe for camping. Savor the tastes and textures of the fresh vegetables in this simple, wholesome stew.

Serves 6 | Prep. time 10 min. | Cooking time 45 min.

Ingredients
1 ½ cups fresh green beans, trimmed and snapped
1 ½ cups fresh wax beans, trimmed and snapped
1 ½ cups diced carrot
2 cups cubed new potatoes
½ teaspoon salt
¼ cup salted butter
¼ cup heavy cream
1 tablespoon all-purpose flour
1 cup whole milk
Salt and pepper to taste

Directions
1. Place the beans, carrots, potatoes, and salt in a saucepan and add just enough water to cover.
2. Simmer for 30–40 minutes, until all the vegetables are tender.
3. Stir in the butter and cream.
4. Whisk the flour into the milk and add it to the pot. Cook until thickened and season with salt and pepper to taste.

Nutrition per serving
Calories 199, Fat 12.8 g, Carbs 18.5 g, Sugar 6.0 g, Protein 3.9 g, Sodium 301.5 mg

Tomato Chickpea Soup

This is not your old-fashioned tomato soup! Adjust the heat to your liking in this nutritious vegan meal.

Serves 8 | Prep. time 10 min. | Cooking time 30 min.

Ingredients
¼ cup extra-virgin olive oil
2 medium yellow onions, diced
1 stalk celery, diced
4 cloves garlic, minced
1 bunch kale, trimmed and chopped (about 3 cups)
2 (28-ounce) cans crushed tomatoes
1 quart low-sodium vegetable stock
1 cup basmati rice, rinsed
¼ cup tomato paste
2 (15-ounce) cans chickpeas, drained and rinsed
1 teaspoon salt
½ teaspoon black pepper
Hot sauce or crushed chilies, to taste

Directions
1. In your Dutch oven over 18 coals, warm the oil and sauté the onion and celery for 3–5 minutes. Stir in the garlic and cook until fragrant.
2. Add the kale, and stir a minute or two, until it begins to wilt.
3. Add the tomatoes, vegetable stock, and rice. Bring the mixture to a boil and let it simmer for 15–20 minutes.
4. Add the tomato paste, chickpeas, salt, pepper, and hot sauce. Cook to heat through, and serve.

Nutrition per serving
Calories 323, Fat 9.3 g, Carbs 52.9 g, Sugar 16.8 g,
Protein 11.6 g, Sodium 812.8 mg

Spiced Lentil Soup

Combine the spices at home to make meal prep a breeze with this brightly colored vegan soup.

Serves 4 | Prep. time 5 min. | Cooking time 30 min.

Ingredients
Spice packet
2 teaspoons ground turmeric
1 ½ teaspoons ground cumin
¼ teaspoon cinnamon
½ teaspoon sea salt
½ teaspoon black pepper
Pinch red pepper flakes

2 tablespoons extra virgin olive oil
1 large onion, diced
3 cloves garlic, minced
¾ cup red lentils, rinsed and drained
1 (15-ounce) can diced tomatoes, with juices
1 (15 ounce) can light coconut milk
1 quart low-sodium vegetable broth
3 cups packed baby spinach
1 tablespoon fresh lemon juice

Directions
1. At home, combine the spices in a small, lidded container, and seal.
2. In your Dutch oven over 18 coals, warm the oil and sauté the onion and garlic until tender.
3. Add the spices and the lentils and mix well. Continue cooking for another minute or two, but don't let the spices burn.

49

4. Add the tomatoes, coconut milk, and broth. Bring it to a boil and simmer, uncovered, for 20 minutes, or until the lentils are tender.
5. Add the spinach and lemon juice, and cook until the spinach wilts.

Nutrition per serving
Calories 254, Fat 14.9 g, Carbs 25.4 g, Sugar 4.8 g,
Protein 7.3 g, Sodium 744.3 mg

SNACKS

We know, snacks happen – and when we're burning extra calories camping, boating, fishing, or sitting in a hammock, we need our snacks. Here is a list of quick ideas that are portable, filling, and good for you.

Trail mix. This filling snack is called trail mix because it's filling and portable. Camping trips are a great time to take advantage of the protein, vitamins, and minerals you'll find in nuts, seeds, and dried berries. Of course, this is a very calorie-dense food and it has some saturated fats, so don't overindulge. (Tip: stir some popcorn or dry Chex cereal into your trail mix to increase its snacking mileage!)

Fruit and cheese. We sometimes forget how pleasing it is to pair an apple with some cheddar, or a pear with some Swiss cheese. Did you know figs are great with Gouda? When you're outside in the shade, or maybe sitting by the water, it's the perfect time to revisit this simple and healthy snack.

Whole-grain crackers, vegetables, and hummus. Kids love dipping things, so fill their snack dishes with a selection of carrots, broccoli, and peppers, some crackers, and some hummus. There are so many ways to customize – try wedges of whole wheat pita, cucumber, or cherry tomatoes!

Nut butter with pretzels. Easy dipping and healthy snacking go hand-in-hand with this classic and simple favorite. To add more volume to your nut butter, try combining it with Greek yogurt.

Veggies and dip. We don't even need to mention this classic, but we wanted to point out that many commercial dressings are loaded with unhealthy oils, MSG, preservatives, and too much salt. It's easy to make your own. Try these:

Healthy Homemade Ranch

(makes 4 servings)

½ cup whole fat Greek yogurt
1 teaspoon dried dill weed
1 clove garlic, minced
1 tablespoon Parmesan
½ teaspoon salt
½ teaspoon black pepper

Nutrition per serving (2 tablespoons)
Calories 36, Fat 2.1 g, Carbs 2.5 g, Sugar 1.9 g,
Protein 1.8 g, Sodium 333.5 mg

Healthy Homemade Tzatziki

(makes 4 servings)

½ cup whole fat Greek yogurt
¼ cup grated cucumber (liquid pressed out as much as possible)
1 clove garlic, minced
½ teaspoon salt

Nutrition per serving (2 tablespoons)
Calories 25, Fat 1.8 g, Carbs 2.3 g, Sugar 2.0 g,
Protein 1.2 g, Sodium 309.7 mg

It can be hard to break the junk-food pattern, but with a focus on fun and flavorful foods, you'll hardly miss that bag of potato chips. After all, we love camping, and it's supposed to be good for us! Why ruin that with a lot of unnecessarily unhealthy eating? You can still have your s'mores (of course!) but with the help of these delicious and easy recipes, you won't come home with that draggy feeling from eating poorly.

VEGETARIAN AND SIDES

Foil Pack Light Blooming Onion

Forget about that deep-fried chain restaurant favorite. This easy campfire recipe is healthier and so easy to prepare.

Serves 4 | Prep. time 10 min. | Cooking time 30 min.

Ingredients
4 medium sweet onions
1 tablespoon butter
2 tablespoons Parmesan cheese
2 tablespoons Worcestershire sauce (or barbecue sauce, or hot sauce)
Salt and pepper to taste

Directions
1. Set out four pieces of aluminum foil and coat them lightly with some butter.
2. Peel the onions and slice them into wedges – taking care not to cut all the way through the bottom. Leave the bottom half-inch intact.
3. Set each onion on a piece of foil and gently pry it open a little.
4. Place a quarter of the butter in the center of each onion. Sprinkle a little Parmesan and a bit of Worcestershire. Season with salt and pepper.
5. Fold the foil around the onions, and wrap tightly.
6. Grill the onions for 30 minutes, or until they are tender.
7. Take care when you're opening the foil, as the steam will be very hot.

Nutrition per serving
Calories 87, Fat 3.8 g, Carbs 11.2 g, Sugar 6.0 g,
Protein 35.9 g, Sodium 870.3 mg

Mango Salsa Stuffed Sweet Potatoes

In this recipe we combine the smooth warmth of a baked sweet potato with the crisp, lively taste of fresh mango salsa.

Serves 4 | Prep. time 15 min. | Cooking time 30–40 min.

Ingredients
For the salsa
1 (15-ounce) can black beans, drained and rinsed
1 large mango, peeled and diced small
½ small red onion, diced
½ cup tomatoes, diced
1 jalapeño pepper, minced
¼ cup chopped cilantro
1 tablespoon extra-virgin olive oil
2 tablespoons lime juice

4 medium sweet potatoes

Directions
1. Prepare the salsa by combining all the ingredients. This can be done ahead of time, but it's best freshly made.
2. Wrap the sweet potatoes in foil and place them near the heat. Turn them often and cook until they're soft, 30–40 minutes.
3. Carefully open the potato packets and slice the potatoes lengthwise. Fluff the flesh with a fork and let them cool enough to eat. Serve with a helping of the salsa on top.

Nutrition per serving
Calories 330, Fat 4.5 g, Carbs 64.8 g, Sugar 13.4 g, Protein 10.9 g, Sodium 21.2 mg

Waldorf Salad

Fresh and tart, this salad makes a great snack or side. It goes very well beside a grilled chicken breast!

Serves 4 | Prep. time 10 min. | Cooking time 0 min.

Ingredients
⅓ cup plain non-fat Greek yogurt
1 tablespoon honey
½ teaspoon salt
¼ teaspoon ground black pepper
2 Granny Smith apples, cored and chopped
1 cup red seedless grapes, halved
1 cup celery, thinly sliced
½ cup chopped toasted walnuts
4–6 leaves romaine lettuce

Directions
1. In a salad bowl, combine the yogurt with the honey, salt, and black pepper.
2. Fold in the apples, grapes, celery, and walnuts.
3. Divide the lettuce among four serving plates, and top with a portion of the salad.

Nutrition per serving
Calories 177, Fat 10.3 g, Carbs 20.5 g, Sugar 17.2 g, Protein 4.8 g, Sodium 326 mg

Quinoa Bean Salad

It has only a few ingredients, but this salad is full of protein, fiber, and healthy omega oils.

Serves 6 | Prep. time 5 min. | Cooking time 0 min.

Ingredients
1 (15-ounce) can kidney beans
2 cups cooked quinoa, cold
1 red onion, minced
½ red bell pepper, minced
2 bunches basil, trimmed and chopped
Juice of 2 lemons
¼ cup extra-virgin olive oil

Directions
1. In a salad bowl, combine the kidney beans, quinoa, red onion, bell pepper, and basil.
2. In a separate bowl or shaker, mix the lemon juice with the olive oil. Mix well, and pour it over the salad. Toss well to combine.

Nutrition per serving
Calories 337, Fat 15.9 g, Carbs 41.1 g, Sugar 4.8 g, Protein 9.7 g, Sodium 329.1 mg

Campfire Pizza Margherita

The beauty of this pizza is the simple blending of its natural flavors. This makes it a perfect choice for outdoor cooking (and eating).

Serves 4 | Prep. time 10 min. | Cooking time 15 min.

Ingredients
For the crust
2 ½ cups all-purpose flour
1 packet rapid rise yeast
1 ½ teaspoons salt
1 cup warm water
5 tablespoons olive oil, divided

Toppings
½ cup plain tomato sauce
6 ounces fresh mozzarella, cut in ¼-inch slices
1 large tomato, sliced
3 tablespoons fresh basil, chopped

Directions
1. Prepare the dough. Combine the flour, yeast, and salt in a mixing bowl. Add the water and 2 tablespoons of the oil, and stir until a ball forms. Knead briefly. (If you like, you can prepare the dough at home. Wrap it tightly in plastic and keep it chilled.)
2. Let it rise for twenty minutes, and divide it in half.
3. Grease a cast iron skillet it with some of the oil. Spread a portion of the dough in the skillet, using your fingertips to press it to the edges. Drizzle a little more oil around the sides.

4. Place the skillet on the grill over medium-high heat. Watch it carefully. After 2–3 minutes, check the bottom to see if it's beginning to brown.
5. When it's golden, carefully remove the skillet from the heat and flip the dough over. Spread it with half the sauce, mozzarella, tomato, and basil.
6. Cover the pan with foil or a lid and return it to the heat. Cook for another 3 minutes, removing the cover in the final minute to let any extra liquid escape.
7. Repeat with the remaining dough and toppings.

Nutrition per serving (half a pizza)
Calories 539, Fat 26.1 g, Carbs 59.4 g, Sugar 1.1 g, Protein 15.8 g, Sodium 1165 mg

Rainbow Salad with Orange Dressing

Summer comes alive in this bowl of crisp and colorful veggies, and the flavors are brightened with the light orange vinaigrette.

Serves 4 | Prep. time 10 min. | Cooking time 0 min.

Ingredients
For the salad
6–8 cups salad greens (such as lettuce, baby spinach, arugula)
1 cup cherry tomatoes, halved
2 carrots, peeped and thinly sliced
4 small radishes, thinly sliced
1 avocado, diced
1 cucumber, thinly sliced
1 yellow pepper, diced

1 cup shredded purple cabbage
½ cup fresh cilantro, chopped

For the dressing
⅓ cup olive oil
2 tablespoons apple cider vinegar
Juice and zest of one orange
1 small shallot, minced

Directions
1. Chop the vegetables and arrange them in a colorful array in a salad bowl.
2. Combine the dressing ingredients in a mason jar and shake well.
3. Serve the salad with a drizzle of the vinaigrette.

Nutrition per serving (half a pizza)
Calories 325, Fat 24.1 g, Carbs 25.0 g, Sugar 9.3 g, Protein 5.9 g, Sodium 115.5 mg

CHICKEN

Hawaiian Chicken Skewers

Pop the chicken into the marinade at home, and you'll have juicy, flavorful chicken at the campsite.

Serves 4 | Prep. time 15 min. plus marinating time | Cooking time 20 min.

Ingredients
For the marinade:
¼ cup soy sauce
¼ cup pineapple juice (from the can)
2 tablespoons brown sugar
1 tablespoon sesame oil
1 teaspoon freshly grated ginger
1 clove garlic, minced

1 ½ pounds boneless, skinless chicken breasts, cut into 2-inch pieces
1 (20-ounce) can pineapple chunks
1 red pepper, cut in 2-inch squares
1 green pepper, cut in 2-inch squares
1 red onion, cut in 2-inch squares

Cooked rice or quinoa, for serving.

Directions

1. Combine the marinade ingredients with the chicken in a resealable bag, and turn to coat. Keep the chicken in the fridge or freezer.
2. When you're ready to cook, remove the chicken from the bag and discard the marinade. If the chicken was frozen, ensure that it has thawed.
3. Heat a grill over medium heat.
4. On your skewers, alternate chicken with pineapple chunks, peppers, and onion.
5. Grill the skewers over medium heat until they are cooked through. Serve with rice or quinoa, if desired.

Nutrition per serving

Calories 361, Fat 5.9 g, Carbs 37.3 g, Sugar 28.5 g,
Protein 41.3 g, Sodium 546.3 mg

Bourbon Grilled Chicken with Salad Greens

This recipe works very well if you pre-marinate the chicken and then pop it in the freezer. You can thaw and grill it at the campsite.

Serves 4 | Prep. time 15 min. plus 1 hour marinating time | Cooking time 20 min.

Ingredients
For the marinade:
½ cup bourbon
¼ cup thawed lemonade concentrate
¼ cup soy sauce
2 tablespoons brown sugar
2 tablespoons apple cider vinegar
2 cloves garlic, minced

4 (6-ounce) chicken breasts

4 cups salad greens, for serving
2 cups hot cooked brown rice, for serving

Directions
1. Combine the marinade ingredients with the chicken in a resealable bag and turn to coat. Let it marinate in the fridge for one hour and then place it in the freezer.
2. At the campsite, allow the chicken to thaw.
3. Heat a grill over medium heat and oil the grate.
4. Drain the marinade into a saucepan and bring it to a boil. Let it simmer on low heat for 5 minutes.

5. Cook the chicken for 4–5 minutes on each side, turning occasionally, and basting often with the sauce. The chicken is done when the internal temperature reaches 165°F.
6. Serve the chicken sliced on a cup of salad greens with half a cup of brown rice.

Nutrition per serving
Calories 446, Fat 5. g, Carbs 38.4 g, Sugar 10.3 g,
Protein 43.0 g, Sodium 1030.9 mg

Dutch Oven Chicken Cacciatore

This simple and aromatic dish is packed with protein and tastes great after a busy day outside. If you like, you can prepare the vegetables at home and bring them to the campsite in a resealable bag for quick meal preparation.

Serves 6-8 | Prep. time 10 min. | Cooking time 30 min.

Ingredients
1 tablespoon olive oil
2 pounds chicken breasts and thighs, diced
1 teaspoon oregano
1 teaspoon basil
½ teaspoon salt
½ teaspoon black pepper
1 small onion, diced
1 red bell pepper cut into thin strips
1 yellow bell pepper cut into thin strips
1 cup sliced mushrooms
3 cloves garlic, minced
1 (20-ounce) can crushed tomatoes
2 cups low-sodium chicken broth
2 ½ cups small dry pasta (like penne)

Directions
1. Place your Dutch oven over medium heat (a 12-inch pot would go over 18 briquettes) and warm the oil. Add the chicken and brown it on all sides. Season it with oregano, basil, salt, and pepper.
2. Add the vegetables and stir. Cook until they begin to soften, stirring often, about 3 minutes.
3. Add the crushed tomatoes, chicken broth, and pasta.

4. Bring the pot to a boil and cover it with the lid. Adjust its position on the coals to keep it simmering for about 20 minutes or until the pasta is cooked, stirring once or twice. Keep the lid off for the last few minutes if the sauce is too runny.

Nutrition per serving
Calories 430, Fat 8.4 g, Carbs 46.0 g, Sugar 8.1 g,
Protein 40.5 g, Sodium 738.9 mg

Avocado Chicken Burger (Paleo)

These tasty chicken patties are loaded with protein and healthy fats. If you follow a paleo diet, eat them on their own or wrapped in lettuce. Other campers can go ahead and use a bun – they're delicious either way.

Serves 4 | Prep. time 10 min. | Cooking time 30 min.

Ingredients
1 pound ground chicken
½ cup spinach, finely chopped
2 tablespoons cilantro, finely chopped
2 tablespoons coconut flour
1 tablespoon olive oil
1 clove garlic, minced
1 teaspoon onion powder
1 teaspoon salt
Pinch red pepper flakes

1 small avocado, diced
Juice of one lime
Butter lettuce leaves (optional)

Directions
1. Combine the ground chicken with the spinach, cilantro, coconut flour, olive oil, garlic, onion powder, salt, and red pepper flakes. (This step can be done at home if you like, kept cold, and brought to the campsite in a sealed container or bag.)
2. Heat the grill over medium heat, and coat it with oil or cooking spray.

3. Gently toss the avocado pieces in the lime juice and fold them in to the chicken mixture.
4. Form 4 patties. Grill them for about 5 minutes per side, or until they're cooked through.

Nutrition per serving
Calories 322, Fat 22.8 g, Carbs 9.3 g, Sugar 1.9 g,
Protein 22.8 g, Sodium 677.4 mg

Dutch Oven Healthy Butter Chicken

The milder flavor of this lighter version of Butter Chicken will be suitable for the whole family, but you can add more heat if you prefer. The cauliflower rice delivers a serving of antioxidants and is loaded with nutrients.

Serves 4 | Prep. time 10 min. | Cooking time 50 min.

Ingredients
For the spice packet
2 teaspoons curry powder
2 teaspoons garam masala
1 teaspoon ground cumin
1 teaspoon ground ginger
½ teaspoon salt
¼ teaspoon cayenne powder

2 tablespoons coconut oil, divided
10 boneless skinless chicken thighs, cut in bite-sized cubes
1 onion, diced
3 cloves garlic, minced
1 (14-ounce) can light coconut milk
1 (6 ounce) can tomato paste

1 head cauliflower, cut into florets
½ cup plain low-fat plain yogurt
½ cup fresh cilantro, chopped (for garnish)

Directions

1. At home, combine the spices in a small lidded container.
2. Place a Dutch oven over 18–20 briquettes and heat 1 tablespoon of the oil.
3. Brown the chicken pieces and sprinkle the spices over them, stirring to combine.
4. Add the onion and garlic and cook another 2 minutes, stirring often.
5. Add the coconut milk and tomato paste and mix well.
6. Cover the pot, and arrange it with 15 briquettes underneath and 8 on top. Try to maintain a temperature around 350°F.
7. Let the chicken simmer for about 45 minutes.
8. Meanwhile, chop the cauliflower until it's the consistency of rice.
9. Heat a cast iron skillet over medium heat and melt the remaining coconut oil.
10. Cook the cauliflower in the oil, stirring often, until it's tender, about 5 minutes.
11. Serve the chicken over the cauliflower with a spoonful of yogurt and a little chopped cilantro.

Nutrition per serving

Calories 450, Fat 19.8 g, Carbs 28.9 g, Sugar 13.9 g,
Protein 43.5 g, Sodium 948.0 mg

Thai Chicken

Serve these delectable chicken thighs with a little brown rice or quinoa. You'll love the blend of sweet and spice in the peanut sauce.

Serves 4 | Prep. time 10 min. | Cooking time 30 min.

Ingredients
For the sauce
½ cup Thai sweet chili sauce
2 tablespoons soy sauce
3 tablespoons creamy peanut butter
2 cloves garlic, minced
1 tablespoon grated ginger
Juice of 1 lime
1 teaspoon Sriracha (or to taste)

2 tablespoons butter
8 bone-in chicken thighs

¼ cup chopped peanuts
Fresh cilantro, chopped

Directions
1. At home, prepare the sauce in a mason jar by combining all the ingredients.
2. At the campsite, in a cast iron skillet over medium-high heat, melt the butter and brown the thighs on both sides.
3. Move the pan to lower heat and pour the sauce over the chicken. Simmer, covered, for 20–25 minutes, or until it's cooked all the way through.
4. Serve with a sprinkle of peanuts and some chopped cilantro.

Nutrition per serving
Calories 376, Fat 21.7 g, Carbs 13.7 g, Sugar 7.8 g, Protein 33.0 g, Sodium 1056.7 mg

FISH AND SEAFOOD

Lemon Salmon Packets

With lemon and fresh dill, these easy foil packets are sure to please all the fish lovers in your family.

Serves 4 | Prep. time 10 min. | Cooking time 30 min.

Ingredients
1 tablespoon butter, softened
4 (6-ounce) salmon fillets
½ teaspoon salt
¼ teaspoon pepper
Pinch cayenne pepper
1 small onion, sliced
4 cloves garlic, sliced
4 fresh dill sprigs
1 medium lemon, sliced

Directions
1. Prepare four squares of foil, double thickness. Spread a little butter in the center of each.
2. Place one piece of fish on each and season them with salt, pepper, and cayenne.
3. Layer on a few rings of onion, a sliced clove of garlic, a sprig of dill, and a portion of the lemon.
4. Fold and seal the packets, leaving a little room for steam to circulate.
5. Cook the packets over medium heat on the grill, shifting them around from time to time.

Nutrition per serving
Calories 305, Fat 19 g, Carbs 3.9 g, Sugar 1.3 g,
Protein 29 g, Sodium 405 mg

73

Blackened Halibut

All it takes is a handful of herbs to transform this fish into something really special. Halibut is packed with micronutrients: selenium, niacin, phosphorus, magnesium, B-vitamins, and more!

Serves 4 | Prep. time 10 min. | Cooking time 10 min.

Ingredients
<u>For the spice packet</u>
2 tablespoons garlic powder
1 tablespoon salt
1 tablespoon onion powder
1 tablespoon dried thyme
1 tablespoon dried oregano
2 teaspoons cayenne pepper
2 teaspoons black pepper
2 teaspoons paprika
1 teaspoon ground cumin

4 (4-ounce) halibut fillets
2 tablespoons butter

Directions
1. At home, combine the spices and place them in a lidded container.
2. At the campsite, heat a cast iron pan over medium heat and melt the butter.
3. Coat the fish with the spices and cook them for 3–5 minutes on each side, depending on the thickness.
4. Remove them from the pan as soon as you can flake the flesh with a fork.

Nutrition per serving
Calories 189, Fat 8.1 g, Carbs 3.4 g, Sugar 1 g,
Protein 24.3 g, Sodium 756.8 mg

Garlic Chili Lime Shrimp

This zesty shrimp is a cinch to prepare! Just toss it in the marinade, and then sauté it to perfection.

Serves 4 | Prep. time 10 min. plus 30 min. marinating time | Cooking time 10 min.

Ingredients
1 pound shrimp, peeled and deveined

For the marinade
½ cup lime juice
Zest of 1 lime
¼ cup olive oil
2 cloves garlic, minced
1 teaspoon chili-garlic paste
1 teaspoon chili powder

½ teaspoon ground cumin
½ teaspoon salt

1 tablespoon butter
¼ cup freshly chopped cilantro
Crushed chilies to taste
1 lime, cut into wedges, for serving

Directions
1. Prepare the marinade by combining all the ingredients. If you like, you can do this at home and bring the marinade to the campsite in a bag large enough to hold the shrimp.
2. At the campsite, add the shrimp to the marinade and let it sit for 30 minutes in a cool place.

3. Heat a skillet over medium heat and melt the butter. Remove the shrimp from the marinade and sauté until it is pink and cooked all the way through.
4. Stir in the cilantro and season with crushed chilies to taste. Serve with lime wedges.

Nutrition per serving
Calories 210, Fat 11 g, Carbs 3.7 g, Sugar 0.6 g, Protein 24 g, Sodium 580 mg

Grilled Trout with Herbs

Lemon and dill are the perfect complement to many fish dishes, and grilled trout by the campfire is certainly no exception.

Serves 4 | Prep. time 10 min. | Cooking time 15 min.

Ingredients
4 (¾-pound) whole trout, cleaned and scaled
2 tablespoons coconut oil
2 cloves garlic, minced
1 bunch dill, chopped (about ½ cup)
1 bunch parsley, chopped (about 1 cup)
Zest and juice of one lemon
½ teaspoon salt
½ teaspoon black pepper
1 lemon, sliced, for serving

Directions
1. Preheat the grill over medium and prepare four pieces of foil large enough to wrap the fish. Give them a light coating of oil or cooking spray.
2. Slash the sides of each fish a few times and rub them with coconut oil.
3. Combine the garlic, dill, parsley, lemon zest and juice, salt, and pepper in a mixing bowl and stir to combine. Fill the cavity of each fish with some of the mixture and top with lemon slices.
4. Wrap each fish tightly in the foil and place the packets on the grill. Cook for about 15 minutes over gentle heat, flipping occasionally. The fish is done when it comes off the bone easily.

Nutrition per serving
Calories 322, Fat 16.8 g, Carbs 1.7 g, Sugar 0.1 g,
Protein 39.6 g, Sodium 395.3 mg

Mussels in Wine Sauce

This might sound like a restaurant-quality meal, and it is! However, it's easy enough to whip up in your Dutch oven, and it's a perfect meal for beach camping.

Serves 4 | Prep. time 10 min. | Cooking time 15 min.

Ingredients
2 tablespoons olive oil
1 medium onion, chopped
3 cloves garlic, sliced
2 tablespoons tomato paste
½ cup white wine
Salt and pepper to taste
4 pounds mussels, debearded and scrubbed

Directions
1. Place a Dutch oven over 18–20 briquettes and heat the oil.
2. Add the onion and cook for 2–3 minutes before stirring in the garlic. Cook a minute more.
3. Add the tomato paste and whisk it in. Cook for about 3 minutes, until the sauce begins to darken.
4. Add the wine and bring the mixture to a boil. Cook until it reduces a little, another minute or two.
5. Add half a cup of water and the mussels. Cover the pot and cook for 10–13 minutes, stirring occasionally, until the mussels have opened. Discard any that do not.
6. Serve the mussels with a portion of the broth.

Nutrition per serving
Calories 295, Fat 11.9 g, Carbs 13.2 g, Sugar 2.4 g, Protein 27.8 g, Sodium 483 mg

PORK

Pork, Apple, and Sweet Potato Skillet

This easy, one-pot dish saves you on clean-up, and it's a cut above your average grilled chop.

Serves 4 | Prep. time 10 min. | Cooking time 30 min.

Ingredients
2 tablespoons butter
4 (4-ounce) boneless pork loin chops
¼ teaspoon salt
¼ teaspoon black pepper
2 medium sweet potatoes, peeled and diced
⅓ cup apple juice
½ teaspoon dried thyme
1 medium apple, peeled and sliced
¼ cup sliced green onions
2 tablespoons honey
½ cup non-fat Greek yogurt

Directions
1. Heat a cast iron skillet or Dutch oven over medium-high heat and melt the butter.
2. Add the pork chops and season them with salt and pepper. Turn them to brown on both sides.
3. Add the sweet potatoes, apple juice, and thyme. Cover and simmer for 10 minutes.
4. Add the apple and green onion and cook 10 more minutes, until the pork is cooked through.

5. Combine the honey and Greek yogurt.
6. Serve the pork, potatoes, and apples with a drizzle of the pan sauce and yogurt mixture.

Nutrition per serving
Calories 365, Fat 10.5 g, Carbs 33.1 g, Sugar 17.9 g, Protein 33.9 g, Sodium 256.1 mg

Cajun Pork Loin

This succulent pork loin cooks up beautifully in your Dutch oven. Prepare at home for a mess-free meal.

Serves 8 | Prep. time 20 min. | Cooking time 2 hours

Ingredients
For the spice rub
1 teaspoon cayenne pepper
1 teaspoon dried oregano
½ teaspoon salt
½ teaspoon ground black pepper
½ teaspoon dried thyme
½ teaspoon ground mustard
3 cloves garlic, minced

1 (4 pound) pork loin roast

Vegetables
4 carrots, peeled and chopped
2 stalks celery, chopped
1 large onion, chopped
4 cloves garlic, chopped
1 small zucchini, chopped

1 tablespoon olive oil
½ cup chicken broth
3 tablespoons all-purpose flour

Directions

1. At home, prepare the spice rub and massage it all over the roast. Wrap the meat tightly in plastic wrap and keep it cold. (Use it within 3 days.)
2. Prepare the vegetables at home and place them in a resealable bag. Refrigerate these as well.
3. When you are ready to bake the roast, prepare a Dutch oven over medium heat (15–18 briquettes underneath).
4. Warm the oil and brown the roast on all sides.
5. Pour the vegetables in the pot around the meat and add the chicken broth.
6. Cover the pot, and arrange it with 8 briquettes underneath and 15 on top. Aim to maintain a temperature of 325°F.
7. Bake for two hours or until the meat is cooked through.
8. Remove the meat and vegetables to plates and keep them warm. Whisk the flour into the pan sauces and serve the gravy over the meat.

Nutrition per serving

Calories 504, Fat 22.2 g, Carbs 8.7 g, Sugar 2.9 g, Protein 63.6 g, Sodium 331.4 mg

Honey Mustard Pork Chops

There's a surprise ingredient in these chops that kicks the whole meal into taste overdrive: peaches! That's right, just a spoonful of peach preserves elevates the tart/sweet combo that honey mustard lovers crave.

Serves 4 | Prep. time 10 min. | Cooking time 12 min.

Ingredients
For the marinade
¼ cup peach preserves
½ cup prepared honey mustard sauce
2 tablespoons lemon juice
Pinch red pepper flakes

4 (6-ounce) lean pork chops

Optional: additional honey mustard sauce and/or peach preserves for serving

Directions
1. At home, combine the marinade ingredients in a resealable bag and mix well.
2. Add the pork chops and turn to coat. Seal the bag and place it in the fridge or freezer.
3. At the campsite, thaw the pork if it's frozen. Remove the meat from the bag and discard the marinade.
4. Heat a grill over medium and oil the grate.
5. Cook the chops for 4–6 minutes per side, until the internal temperature reaches 165°F. Let the meat rest for 5 minutes before serving.

Nutrition per serving
Calories 504, Fat 22.2 g, Carbs 8.7 g, Sugar 2.9 g, Protein 63.6 g, Sodium 331.4 mg

Kielbasa Potato Hash

With lean pork kielbasa and just one pan, you can turn out this colorful and satisfying dish in just twenty minutes!

Serves 4 | Prep. time 10 min. | Cooking time 30 min.

Ingredients
1 tablespoon olive oil
2 large potatoes, peeled and diced
12 ounces lean pork kielbasa, cut into 1/4" rounds
1 green bell pepper, diced
½ yellow, red or orange bell pepper, diced
1 medium onion, diced

Directions
1. While you peel the potatoes, heat a large cast iron skillet or Dutch oven over medium-high heat and warm the oil.
2. Add the potatoes and cook until they are golden, about 10 minutes, stirring from time to time.
3. Meanwhile, prepare the other ingredients and add them to the pot. Cook until everything is browned and tender. Serve hot.

Nutrition per serving
Calories 317, Fat 11.1 g, Carbs 39.4 g, Sugar 6.0 g, Protein 17.4 g, Sodium 796.2 mg

Pork Loin with Herbs

In this recipe, we treat the humble pork loin to a handful of herbs. The pan sauce is so good – don't forget to spoon a little over the meat when you serve.

Serves 4 | Prep. time 10 min. | Cooking time 1 hour.

Ingredients

1 ½ pounds pork loin
1 tablespoon olive oil
1 teaspoon dried basil
1 teaspoon dried marjoram
1 teaspoon dried thyme
1 teaspoon rubbed sage
1 teaspoon black pepper
½ teaspoon sea salt

2 tablespoons olive oil
¾ cup water
12 baby potatoes, scrubbed
2 tablespoons cornstarch in 2 tablespoons water

Directions

1. At home, rub the roast with olive oil. Combine all the spices, and rub them onto the surface of the meat. Wrap it tightly in plastic wrap and keep it refrigerated.
2. In a Dutch oven over 18 briquettes, heat the oil. Place the roast in the hot pot, turning it from time to time to brown it on all sides.
3. Pour the water in around the roast, and arrange the potatoes inside.
4. Cover the pot and arrange it with 8 briquettes underneath and 16 on top. Try to maintain a temperature of 350°F.

5. After 45 minutes, check the roast to see if the internal temperature has reached 165°F. If it has, remove it (and the potatoes) to a plate and cover it with foil.
6. Whisk the cornstarch and water and add them to the pan sauce. Stir well and cook until it's thickened and reduced slightly.
7. Slice and serve the roast with a portion of the potatoes and a drizzle of the gravy.

Nutrition per serving

Calories 607, Fat 22.6 g, Carbs 63.8 g, Sugar 3.4 g, Protein 39.0 g, Sodium 920.3 mg

BEEF

Healthy Joe Stuffed Peppers

These tasty peppers are filled with a lightened-up sloppy joe mix, and they heat up nicely in foil packets – or you can use your cast iron skillet or Dutch oven.

Serves 4 | Prep. time 25 min. | Cooking time 30 min.

Ingredients

1 pound lean ground beef
1 medium yellow onion, chopped
3 cloves garlic, minced
1 teaspoon Italian seasoning
½ teaspoon chili powder
1 cup tomato sauce
¼ cup ketchup
1 tablespoon tomato paste
1 tablespoon Worcestershire sauce
1 tablespoon brown sugar
4 bell peppers, tops removed and cored
½ cup shredded Monterey Jack
½ cup water
Chopped green onions, for garnish

Directions

1. In a skillet over medium-high heat, brown the beef. Drain any excess fat.
2. Add the onion and cook until it is softened, about 5 minutes. Stir in the garlic and cook until fragrant. Stir in the Italian seasoning and chili powder.

3. Add the tomato sauce, ketchup, tomato paste, Worcestershire sauce, and brown sugar. Mix well.
4. If you're preparing the filling ahead, cool and refrigerate it in a lidded container.
5. Spoon the filling into the peppers. Wrap each tightly in foil, or arrange them in a cast iron skillet or Dutch oven. If you're using a skillet or Dutch oven, add ½ cup of water, and cover tightly.
6. Place the foil packets near the fire and turn them from time to time (keeping them upright). The pan or pot should go over medium heat. Bake for about 30 minutes, checking them often.
7. When the peppers are tender and the meat is heated through, sprinkle a portion of cheese on each one. Cook to melt the cheese, and serve with some chopped green onion.

Nutrition per serving
Calories 320, Fat 12 g, Carbs 29.2 g, Sugar 6.8 g,
Protein 28.1 g, Sodium 748.3 mg

Unconstructed Healthy Cabbage Rolls

With all of the taste and a fraction of the work, this simple dish delivers a dose of anti-oxidants, fiber, and protein everyone can enjoy.

Serves 4 | Prep. time 10 min. | Cooking time 30 min.

Ingredients
1 pound extra-lean ground beef (95% lean)
1 large onion, diced
2 teaspoons Italian seasoning
½ teaspoon salt
½ teaspoon black pepper
1 (28-ounce) can diced tomatoes with juices
1 (8-ounce) can tomato sauce
1 small head cabbage, thinly sliced (about 6 cups)
½ green pepper, thinly sliced
4 cups hot cooked brown rice

Directions
1. In a skillet over medium-high heat, heat the oil and brown the beef. Drain any excess fat.
2. In a separate pot, prepare the rice according to the package instructions.
3. Add the onion and cook until it is softened, about 5 minutes. Stir in the Italian seasoning, salt, and pepper.
4. Add the diced tomatoes and tomato sauce. Bring it to a simmer and add the cabbage and green pepper.

5. Cook, covered, for about 10 minutes, then remove the lid and cook another 5–8 minutes until the liquid has reduced and the cabbage is tender.
6. Serve the cabbage mixture over a cup of brown rice.

Nutrition per serving
Calories 660, Fat 20.2 g, Carbs 70.9 g, Sugar 13.7 g, Protein 41.6 g, Sodium 1030 mg

Broccoli and Beef Skillet

The trick to a healthy beef dish is almost always portion control. We increase the proportion of vegetables and serve over a bed of steaming quinoa. The vegetables should be bright and crisp, so be careful not to overcook them.

Serves 4 | Prep. time 25 min. | Cooking time 30 min.

Ingredients
For the marinade
½ cup low-sodium soy sauce
1 tablespoon Worcestershire sauce
1 (1-inch) thumb fresh ginger, grated
2 cloves garlic, minced
2 tablespoons honey
½ teaspoon red pepper flakes

1 pound top sirloin steak, cut in bite-sized strips

2 tablespoons olive oil, divided
2 large carrots, peeled and chopped
1 large onion, diced
4–5 cups broccoli florets, trimmed

1 cup water
2 tablespoons cornstarch
2 cups hot quinoa, cooked

Directions
1. At home, place the marinade ingredients in a resealable bag and mix well. Add the beef strips and turn to coat. Place the bag in the fridge or freezer.
2. At the campsite, rinse and cook the quinoa.

3. Place a 14-inch skillet over medium heat. Add 1 tablespoon of olive oil and the carrots, and cook for 3–4 minutes.
4. Add the other vegetables and cook until they are crisp-tender. Remove them to a bowl, cover, and keep them warm.
5. Add the remaining oil to the pan and increase the heat to medium-high. Remove the beef strips from the marinade (keep the marinade) and cook them quickly, being careful not to crowd the pan.
6. As they are cooked, remove the beef strips to the bowl with the vegetables.
7. When the beef is done, mix the cornstarch and water into the marinade and add it to the pan. Cook, stirring, until it has boiled and reduced, 3–4 minutes.
8. Add the meat and vegetables back to the sauce and stir to coat them and heat through.
9. Serve over a portion of the hot quinoa.

Nutrition per serving
Calories 534, Fat 12.4 g, Carbs 59 g, Sugar 17.5 g, Protein 46.7 g, Sodium 1328.7 mg

Sriracha and Scallion Sirloin

Warm up the grill and your taste buds with this flavorful and lean cut of beef.

Serves 4 | Prep. time 5 min. plus 2–4 hours marinating time | Cooking time 6–10 min.

Ingredients
For the marinade
2 tablespoons sriracha
2 tablespoons soy sauce
2 tablespoons olive oil
1 tablespoon brown sugar
1 bunch scallions, minced

1 pound top sirloin steak

Directions
1. At home, place the marinade ingredients in a resealable bag and mix well. Add the steaks and turn to coat. Place the bag in the fridge or freezer. (If you choose to do this step at the campsite, chill the steaks in the marinade for 3–5 hours.)
2. At the campsite, remove the steaks from the marinade, and discard the marinade.
3. Oil the grill and heat it to medium high.
4. Grill the steaks for 3–5 minutes per side, depending on the thickness of the meat and the desired doneness.
5. Let the meat rest for 5 minutes before serving.

Nutrition per serving
Calories 254, Fat 11.1 g, Carbs 1.5 g, Sugar 0.9 g, Protein 35.0 g, Sodium 232.0 mg

Teriyaki Steak Skewers

We're big on preparing things at home for an easy time at the campsite, but you do it your way! We suggest putting the steak into its marinade at home, for less mess at the campsite.

Serves 6 | Prep. time 20 min. | Cooking time 20 min.

Ingredients
2 pounds sirloin steak, cut in ¼" strips across the grain

For the marinade
½ cup low-sodium soy sauce
3 tablespoons honey
3 cloves garlic, minced
1 tablespoon freshly grated ginger

2 tablespoons sesame seeds
4 stalks green onion, chopped

Optional: salad greens or brown rice for serving

Directions
1. Prepare the marinade by combining all the ingredients in a resealable bag. Add the beef strips and turn to coat. Marinate for 30–45 minutes, or do this step at home and place the bag in the freezer.
2. When you're ready to cook, preheat a grill to high. Pour the marinade into a saucepan (add a little water if needed) and thread the beef strips onto skewers.
3. Simmer the marinade while you grill the meat. Brush the skewers from time to time with the marinade, and be careful not to overcook the meat.
4. Serve with a sprinkle of sesame seeds and green onion.

Nutrition per serving
Calories 354, Fat 12.1 g, Carbs 10.7 g, Sugar 8.7 g,
Protein 47.4 g, Sodium 867.2 mg

DESSERTS

Oatmeal Cranberry Baked Apples

You might want to make double of these tasty foil-pack baked apples, because with this recipe it's OK to have seconds!

Serves 4 | Prep. time 10 min. | Cooking time 20 min.

Ingredients
4 medium apples
2 tablespoons butter (or coconut oil)
1 tablespoon almond butter
2 tablespoons dried cranberries, chopped
3 tablespoons rolled oats
½ teaspoon cinnamon
2 tablespoons brown sugar
¼ cup chopped pecans

Directions
1. Lay out four pieces of foil, and lightly coat each with butter or coconut oil.
2. Wash and core the apples (don't slice or chop them), being careful not to pierce the bottom.
3. In a small bowl, combine the butter, almond butter, cranberries, rolled oats, cinnamon, brown sugar, and pecans. Mix well.
4. Divide mixture among the apples, pressing it down into the cavity.
5. Wrap the apples in the foil and place them near the fire or directly on the grill. Cook for about 20 minutes, until softened.

Nutrition per serving
Calories 187, Fat 13.7 g, Carbs 18.2 g, Sugar 11.0 g, Protein 1.9 g, Sodium 43.3 mg

Grilled Fruit Skewers

The kids can skewer up all their favorites and grill them while you prepare the yummy yogurt dip!

Serves 4 | Prep. time 10 min. | Cooking time 10 min.

Ingredients
4 cups mixed fruit: strawberries, pineapple, peaches, bananas, nectarines, plums

<u>For the dip</u>
1 cup fat-free vanilla Greek yogurt
2 tablespoons honey
¼ teaspoon cinnamon

Wooden skewers, soaked in water

Directions
1. Heat a clean grill to medium.
2. Thread the fruit onto the skewers and place them on the grill. Cook for about 5 minutes, and then turn them. Cook another 2–3 minutes.
3. Meanwhile, combine the ingredients for the dip.
4. Serve and enjoy!

Nutrition per serving
Calories 150, Fat 0.5 g, Carbs 33.2 g, Sugar 26.5 g, Protein 5.4 g, Sodium 17.9 mg

Dreamy Chocolate Pudding

This pudding is so creamy and delicious you'd never know it's made with low-fat milk!

Serves 6 | Prep. time 10 min. | Cooking time 15 min.

Ingredients
½ cup sugar
3 tablespoons cornstarch
¼ cup cocoa powder
½ teaspoon salt
2 ½ cups 1% low-fat milk
½ cup evaporated fat-free milk
2 ounces (60% cocoa) bittersweet chocolate finely chopped (about ¼ cup)
1 teaspoon vanilla extract

Directions
1. In a heavy saucepan, combine the sugar, cornstarch, cocoa, and salt. Whisk them together and gradually stir in the milk and evaporated milk.
2. Bring it to a boil over medium-high heat, then reduce the heat and simmer for a minute or two, until thickened.
3. Remove the pot from the heat and mix in the chocolate and vanilla. Stir until smooth.
4. Divide the pudding into 6 serving dishes and chill for 4 hours. If you want to prevent a film on the top, cover them with plastic wrap touching the surface of the pudding.

Nutrition per serving
Calories 179, Fat 4.0 g, Carbs 31.8 g, Sugar 27.4 g, Protein 5.5 g, Sodium 263.5 mg

Lemon Blueberry Dutch Baby

Break out the Dutch oven for this Dutch baby! We've reduced the sugar and butter jut a little to lighten up this dish, and the lemon and blueberries add a burst of flavor.

Serves 4 | Prep. time 10 min. | Cooking time 30 min.

Ingredients
1 pint fresh blueberries
1 teaspoon sugar
Juice of 1 lemon
Zest of half a lemon
2 eggs
½ cup 1% milk
½ cup all-purpose flour
⅛ teaspoon nutmeg
Pinch salt
2 tablespoons butter

Directions
1. In a mixing bowl, combine the blueberries, sugar, lemon, and lemon zest. Stir and let it sit for 10–15 minutes.
2. Heat a 10 or 12" Dutch oven over 18 briquettes.
3. In a separate bowl, beat the eggs and stir in the milk. Add the flour, nutmeg, and salt, and stir just to combine.
4. Melt the butter in the Dutch oven and pour in the batter. Cover the pot and place 8 briquettes on top. You're aiming for a temperature of 425°F.
5. Bake for 30 minutes, or until the batter is all cooked.
6. Serve a portion of the Dutch baby with a spoonful of blueberry sauce.

Nutrition per serving
Calories 198, Fat 8.5 g, Carbs 25.1 g, Sugar 10.2 g,
Protein 6.3 g, Sodium 384.9 mg

Healthy Dutch Oven Berry Cobbler

No camping recipe book feels complete without a Dutch oven cobber, and we have not failed you! These berries are loaded with fiber, nutrients, and anti-oxidants, and they help fight inflammation.

Serves 8 | Prep. time 15 min. | Cooking time 35 min.

Ingredients

For the filling
1 ½ cups blueberries
1 ½ cups raspberries
1 ½ cups blackberries
2 cups sliced strawberries
1 teaspoon cinnamon
½ cup sugar
2 tablespoons cornstarch

For the topping
1 ½ cups flour
⅓ cup sugar
2 teaspoons baking powder
½ teaspoon salt
5 tablespoons cold butter, cubed
½ cup 1% milk

Directions

1. Combine the filling ingredients and mix well. Let them sit for at least an hour.
2. In a mixing bowl, combine the flour, sugar, baking powder, and salt. Cut in the butter until the mixture forms a coarse meal. Stir in the milk until a dough forms. Knead it lightly. You can choose to roll it out and cut biscuits if you like.

3. Heat a 14" Dutch oven over 12 coals. Pour the berry mixture into the pot.
4. Spoon scoops of the dough onto the berries, or arrange your cut biscuits on top.
5. Cover the pot and arrange 18 coals on top.
6. Cook for about 35 minutes, turning the pot every five minutes, until the topping is cooked.
7. Let it sit for 30 minutes before serving.

Nutrition per serving

Calories 316, Fat 8.1 g, Carbs 59.0 g, Sugar 50.8 g, Protein 4.3 g, Sodium 393.9 mg

Healthy No-Bake Cheesecake

Top this with your favorite fruit or sauce, if you like. This gluten free dessert comes in at under 150 calories per serving!

Serves 12 | Prep. time 15 min. | Cooking time 0 min.

Ingredients
For the crust
½ cup almond meal
2 tablespoons almond butter
2 tablespoons brown sugar
1 tablespoon milk

For the filling
2 (8-ounce) packages light cream cheese
1 cup 2% Greek yogurt
2 tablespoons sugar
1 tablespoon lemon juice
2 teaspoons vanilla extract
Pinch salt

Directions
1. Combine the crust ingredients and mix well. Press them into a 9" pie plate or dish.
2. Mix the filling ingredient together and spread them in the pie plate.
3. Chill for 2–3 hours, and serve!

Nutrition per serving
Calories 147, Fat 9.5 g, Carbs 10.1 g, Sugar 7.9 g, Protein 5.6 g, Sodium 173.9 mg

Also by Louise Davidson

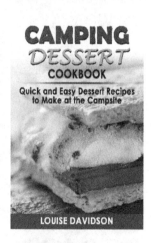

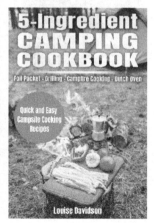

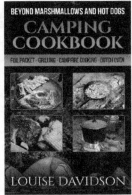

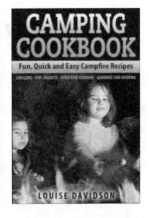

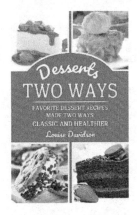

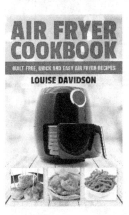

RECIPE INDEX

APPENDIX

Cooking Conversion Charts

1. Measuring Equivalent Chart

Type	Imperial	Imperial	Metric
Weight	1 dry ounce		28g
	1 pound	16 dry ounces	0.45 kg
Volume	1 teaspoon		5 ml
	1 dessert spoon	2 teaspoons	10 ml
	1 tablespoon	3 teaspoons	15 ml
	1 Australian tablespoon	4 teaspoons	20 ml
	1 fluid ounce	2 tablespoons	30 ml
	1 cup	16 tablespoons	240 ml
	1 cup	8 fluid ounces	240 ml
	1 pint	2 cups	470 ml
	1 quart	2 pints	0.95 l
	1 gallon	4 quarts	3.8 l
Length	1 inch		2.54 cm

* Numbers are rounded to the closest equivalent

Internal Temperature for Meats

Beef, Lamb, Roasts, Pork, Veal, Ham

Rare	120 – 130°F (49 – 54°C)
Medium Rare	130 – 135°F (54 – 57°C)
Medium	135 – 145°F (57 – 63°C)
Medium Well	145 – 155°F (64 – 68°C)
Well Done	155°F and greater (68°C)

Pork, ribs

Fully Cooked	190 – 205°F (88 – 96°C)

Poultry

Fully Cooked	At least 165°F (74°C)

Fish

Fully Cooked	At least 130°F (54°C)

Made in the USA
Middletown, DE
05 November 2023

42025101R00066